PURITAN ECONOMIC
EXPERIMENTS

Other books by Gary North

Marx's Religion of Revolution, 1968 [1988]
An Introduction to Christian Economics, 1973
Unconditional Surrender, 1981
Successful Investing in an Age of Envy, 1981
The Dominion Covenant: Genesis, 1982
Government By Emergency, 1983
The Last Train Out, 1983
Backward, Christian Soldiers?, 1984
75 Bible Questions Your Instructors Pray You Won't Ask, 1984
Coined Freedom: Gold in the Age of the Bureaucrats, 1984
Moses and Pharaoh: Dominion Religion Versus Power Religion, 1985
Negatrends, 1985
The Sinai Strategy, 1986
Conspiracy: A Biblical View, 1986
Unholy Spirits: Occultism and New Age Humanism, 1986
Honest Money, 1986
Fighting Chance, 1986 [with Arthur Robinson]
Dominion and Common Grace, 1987
Inherit the Earth, 1987
The Pirate Economy, 1987
Liberating Planet Earth, 1987
Healer of the Nations, 1987
Is the World Running Down?, 1988
Tools of Dominion, 1988

Books edited by Gary North

Foundations of Christian Scholarship, 1976
Tactics of Christian Resistance, 1983
The Theology of Christian Resistance, 1983
Editor, *Journal of Christian Reconstruction* (1974-1981)

PURITAN ECONOMIC EXPERIMENTS

Gary North

Institute for Christian Economics
Tyler, Texas

Published in Tyler, Texas
by the Institute for Christian Economics

Distributed by Dominion Press, Fort Worth, Texas

Typesetting by Nhung Pham Nguyen

Printed in the United States of America

ISBN 0-930464-14-1

This book is dedicated to

Paul Poirot

the best editor I ever saw.

TABLE OF CONTENTS

PREFACE

The bulk of this little book appeared originally in a series of three articles in *The Freeman* in the spring of 1974. They, in turn, grew out of my doctoral dissertation, "The Concept of Property in Puritan New England, 1630-1720." The dissertation, except for Chapter Two on medieval economics, has been published piecemeal over the years. The chapters on New England's Puritan economic thought and practice appeared in *The Journal of Christian Reconstruction*, Vol. V (Winter 1978-79) and Vol. VI (Summer 1979 and Winter 1979-80). The dissertation's first chapter, on biblical economics, appeared as Chapter Eighteen of *An Introduction to Christian Economics* (Craig Press, 1973), "An Outline of Biblical Economic Thought." Finally, the dissertation's chapter on Max Weber appeared in *The Journal of Christian Reconstruction*, Vol. III (Summer 1976), as "The 'Protestant Ethic' Hypothesis." Thus, for any reader who becomes serious about pursuing some of the theological or economic issues raised in this book, the more detailed evidence is available, though no doubt out of date in terms of the latest findings, claims, and interpretations of professional historians. But who knows? Maybe the professionals are all wrong anyway. In any case, I think it is better to get this material back into print than to wait until I have spare time to update it extensively. I have long given up hope of finding spare time to update old material extensively. There is too much new material to write.

INTRODUCTION

This book is relatively simple. It covers three topics: the common ownership of land, the imposition of price and wage controls, and sumptuary legislation. The final topic is unfamiliar to most people. Three centuries ago, legislators believed that it was the civil government's duty to enforce fashions. Sumptuary laws were not aimed at public lewdness; rather, they were aimed at members of the lower class who wore clothing appropriate to the upper class. The legislators recognized that clothing was (and usually is) symbolic of personal status within a social hierarchy. They then jumped from the social hierarchy to the hierarchy of civil government. Rather than allowing market forces (mainly income and expenditure restraints) to "keep the lower class in its place," they resorted to public coercion.

By restricting this book to these three topics, I have done my best to present the Puritan economic world-and-life view in terms that can be readily grasped. I have also shown why their attempts to enforce this economic worldview by resorting to the sword of civil government was based, not on biblical revelation, but rather on a specific inherited intellectual tradition: early scholasticism. While it may seem strange that Protestants as radical as the New England Puritans were in fact followers of Thomas Aquinas in the field of economics, there were reasons for it. First, they were not familiar with the later scholastic

1

tradition, which was much more free market oriented.[1] Second, the Puritans never fully broke with the theory of natural law, and it was the scholastics who had imported and baptized this humanist myth of ancient Greece and Rome. The Puritans did not attempt to rethink economics in terms of the Bible; instead, they simply imported medieval scholastic economic categories into their legislation regarding pricing.

Their land policies were governed by their desire to maintain the tight control of the two local community institutions of church and state. They believed that geography reinforces ethics. They designed each town to place the church at the center. They did what they could to restrict the spreading out of families across the landscape. They kept large parts of the town in commons — areas that were supposed to substitute for the amassing of large privately owned tracts of land that would lead to the dispersal of families. They saw land hunger as an anti-social force. It was seen as a kind of centrifugal force that would lead to the atomization of the towns. They much preferred to spin off whole new villages rather than spin off families one by one.

The same sort of impulse was reflected in fashion, they believed. What was needed was hierarchy — a hierarchy that would be reflected in what people wore. Again, they feared confusion that is created by economic change, which inevitably asserts itself in the form of social change. They saw hierarchy as social, political, and economic. They believed for half a century that they could preserve social hierarchy by means of the political hierarchy: restricting the economy by law.

The period 1630-1720 was a period of great experimentation, an economic, social, and political laboratory in the New England wilderness. That experiment transformed the wilderness, and in

---

1. Alejandro A. Chafuen, *Christians for Freedom: Late-Scholastic Economics* (San Francisco: Ignatius, 1986); Marjorie Grice-Hutchinson, *The School of Salamanca: Readings in Spanish Monetary Theory, 1544-1605* (Oxford: The Clarendon Press, 1952); Murray N. Rothbard, "Late Medieval Origins of Free Market Economic Thought," *Journal of Christian Reconstruction*, II (Summer 1975), pp. 62-75.

doing so, also transformed Puritanism. This had not been the intention of the founders, though it had always been their great fear.[2] When Puritan optimism regarding New England's earthly future began to fade after 1660, and then their economic experiments failed after King Philip's War in 1675-76, a new worldview steadily began to replace the older Puritanism, a combination of pietism and natural law theory that still dominates Christian social thought. There is no better way to see how the Puritan worldview failed to meet the challenge, not of the wilderness but of prosperity, than to examine their three major economic experiments: government controls on land, prices, and fashions.

---

2. Sacvan Bercovich, *The American Jeremiad* (Madison: University of Wisconsin Press, 1978), ch. 1.

1

COMMON OWNERSHIP

The experience that was had in this common course and condition, tried sundry years, and that amongst godly and sober men, may well evince the vanity of that conceit of Plato's and other ancients, applauded by some of later times, that the taking away of property, and bringing in community into a commonwealth, would make them happy and flourishing; as if they were wiser than God.

William Bradford [1]

One of the more familiar incidents in American history, at least within conservative circles, is the disastrous experiment with a common storehouse in the Pilgrim colony in 1621-23. Nearly half the 102 passengers on the *Mayflower* died of cold, sickness, and hunger during the first winter of 1620-21.[2] A fire in January destroyed the common storehouse and some of their meager supplies.[3] In the fall, a second ship, the *Fortune*, arrived with 36 poverty-stricken settlers. Those already settled in Plymouth had to provide for them. The colonists went on half rations. Governor Bradford warned that this new burden would

---

1. William Bradford, "History 'Of Plimoth Plantation,'" in Joseph Allan Montgomery (ed.), *Christian History of the Constitution of the United States of America* (San Francisco: American Christian Constitution Press, 1960), p. 213. Compiled by Verna Hall. I have modernized the spelling.

2. George D. Langdon, Jr., *Pilgrim Colony: A History of New Plymouth, 1620-1691* (New Haven, Connecticut: Yale University Press, 1966), p. 14.

3. *Idem.*

threaten the colony with famine. In the spring of 1622, this prophecy came true.[4]

The Common Storehouse

What is perhaps the Pilgrims' second-best-known historical incident after the thanksgiving feast is the disastrous experiment with common ownership. Everyone was required to bring all that he had produced into the common storehouse, and to each family was rationed out the supplies deemed appropriate to its size. It was a classic experiment with the Communist principle announced by Karl Marx: "From each according to his ability, to each according to his needs!"[5] It did not work. It intensified the famine. Governor Bradford describes in some detail in his history of the colony how young men refused to work in the common fields.

For this community [of property—G.N.] (so far as it was) was found to breed much confusion and discontent, and retard much employment that would have been to their benefit and comfort. For the young men that were most able and fit for labor and service did repine that they should spend their time and strength to work for other men's wives and children, without any recompense. The strong, or man of parts, had no more in the division of victuals and clothes than he that was weak and not able to do a quarter the other could; this was thought injustice. The aged and graver men to be ranked and equalized in labors, and victuals, and clothes, etc., with the meaner and younger sort, thought it some indignity and disrespect unto them. And for men's wives to be commanded to do service for other men, as dressing their meat, washing their clothes, etc., they deemed it a kind of slavery, neither could many husbands well brook it.[6]

Upon petition of the planters in 1623, the Governor and his

---

4. *Ibid.*, p. 17.

5. Karl Marx, "Critique of the Gotha Program" (1875), in Karl Marx and Frederick Engels, *Selected Works*, 3 vols. (Moscow: Progress Publishers, 1970), III, p. 19.

6. Bradford's "History," *op. cit.*, p. 213.

council decided to follow their advice: to assign families their personal plots of farm land (according to family size) and abolish the common storehouse. Only the tools of the colony were held in common, and land could not be conveyed (initially) by inheritance.[7] Immediately, men and women returned to the harvest fields. Bradford writes: "By this time harvest was come, and instead of famine, now God gave them plenty, and the face of things was changed, to the rejoicing of the hearts of many, for which they blessed God. And the effect of their particular planting was well seen, for all had, one way and other, pretty well to bring the year about, and some of the abler sort and more industrious had to spare, and sell to others, so as any general want or famine hath not been amongst them since to this day."[8] Later, the restriction against deeding land to children was abolished.

An Imposed Decision

What is less known about this incident is how the little colony ever made such a disastrous decision in the first place. The fact of the matter is that the colonists had never wanted to inaugurate a system of totally common storehouse. The group of British "adventurers" that had supplied the Pilgrim exiles in Holland with traveling money and capital had insisted that the colony be made a part of the joint-stock company. The assets of the colony were therefore the assets of the company, headquartered in Britain, and the agricultural products were to be shared equally among company members, both colonial and British. Governor Bradford was the chief agent of the company in New England; hence, he was compelled to impose the common storehouse system.[9]

In the original negotiations, it had been understood that

---

7. Langdon, *Pilgrim Colony*, p. 29.

8. Bradford, *op. cit.*, p. 217.

9. Andrew Lane, "The Pilgrim Fathers were never socialists: An historical reflection," *Review of the News* (Nov. 24, 1976), pp. 35-50.

profits would be shared by all members of the company, but the colonists had not agreed to the sharing of houses, gardens, and other improved land. They were informed of these terms only as they were about to leave for North America, and as they left, they sent back word to the merchant adventurers that their agents who had agreed to such terms had not been empowered to do so.[10] But the continuing dependence upon the company for resources during the first year of the colony's existence compelled them to give in to the company's terms.[11]

The story did not end in 1623, when necessity forced the hands of the colonists. In 1627, the bickering British directors sold out their interests in the colony to the settlers for 1800 pounds. The settlers were to spend a decade and a half in paying off their debt, and at times had to borrow extra time at rates of 30 percent to 50 percent. Nevertheless, they persisted and finally repaid the debt, in 1642.

In 1627, shortly after buying out the British directors, Governor Bradford supervised the division of the colony's assets among the settlers. First, they divided livestock. There were few animals, so the 156 people (fewer than 40 families) were divided into a dozen companies; each company received a cow and two goats. In January of 1628, the land was divided, this time by random lot. Complaints about unequal housing were forestalled by requiring those who received better housing to make an equalizing payment to those receiving poorer housing. Peace was preserved.

There was one decision, however, which was to prove costly. Meadow was in short supply, so it was kept in common ownership. Furthermore, fishing, fowling, and water remained "open" to all settlers.[12] The Pilgrims were to have the same difficulties with the administration of these common fields as their neighbors, the Puritans, were to experience. Only after 1675, when the commons throughout New England were increasingly distrib-

---

10. Langdon, *Pilgrim Colony*, p. 9.

11. *Ibid.*, p. 26.

12. *Ibid.*, p. 31.

uted to the families in each town, were these problems overcome.

Varying Concepts of Ownership

In order to understand the thinking of the first half century of New England's settlers, we have to realize that these immigrants did not bring over from England some universally accepted concept of land ownership. There was an obvious tendency for groups of settlers from one region in England to establish homogeneous townships in Massachusetts. English towns had developed at least three major systems of land tenure: the open field system, the closed field system, and the incorporated borough. All three appeared in New England in the early years.

The open field system stressed the community administration of land. It is this system which we generally associate with the word "medieval," although the Middle Ages saw many systems of land tenure. Sumner Chilton Powell has described these systems in some detail in his Pulitzer Prize-winning study, *Puritan Village.* The open field system "regarded the advantages of the area as communal property, to be shared by all. No one was to exclude a neighbor from such a necessity as good meadow, or the down, or the woods. And if anyone practiced such exclusion, or attempted to increase the amount of his holding at the expense of his neighbors, all villagers reacted instantly to restore their 'rights.'"[13] Needless to say, this approach did not survive long in the setting of New England.

Quite different was an English borough like Berkhamsted. In the early seventeenth century, over one thousand acres "were opened up, bought, or traded, in countless individual transactions. If the men of Berkhamsted were doing nothing else, they were trading land."[14] The legend of the Yankee trader was rooted in this sort of English inheritance. There were some enclosed lands, but most of the farmers were shifting as rapidly

---

13. Sumner Chilton Powell, *Puritan Village: The Formation of a New England Town* (Garden City, New York: Doubleday Anchor, [1963] 1966), p. 11.

14. *Ibid.*, p. 26.

as possible to a system of individual farm management.

A third system was a sort of combination, the closed field system of East Anglia. "There was one common pasture, but each farmer was expected to provide a balance of arable pasture and hay meadow for himself. He succeeded, or failed on his own farming ability."[15] One of the problems in a Massachusetts town like Sudbury was the diversity of backgrounds of its inhabitants. There was no agreement as to where the locus of economic sovereignty should be. Should it be the individual farmer? Should it be the town's selectmen who controlled the resources of the town commons?

Tightly Knit Communities

The towns and colonial governments of seventeenth-century New England were not strictly theocracies; ordained ministers could not be elected to political office. But they were important as advisers. Furthermore, the laymen of that era were very often more theologically motivated than ministers of this century. Most of the towns were regarded as tightly knit Christian commonwealths by their inhabitants, and during the first fifty years of their existence, they imposed restrictions on immigration into the local community. They were concerned that newcomers might not meet the religious and moral standards of the present inhabitants. As late as 1678, the records of Plymouth Colony offered the hope that "the Court will be careful, that whom they accept are persons orthodox in their judgments." The Puritan towns of Boston, Cambridge, Dedham, and probably many others all included the requirement that outsiders be cleared by town officials before they were allowed to buy land locally. Braintree even included a restriction on land sales (though not explicitly religious in intent) that local residents would have the right to bid first on all property offered for sale to outsiders.

It is significant that in the final quarter of the century, these religious restrictions were generally dropped. Instead, a new

---

15. *Ibid.*, p. 72

requirement — in fact, a new emphasis on an old requirement — appeared: restrictions on immigrants who might become a burden on the welfare rolls. The towns had steadily become more pluralistic theologically, but the fear of an increase in tax rates was a truly ecumenical device. By offering economic support to local indigents, the townspeople were afraid that outsiders might take advantage of this legal charity. Barriers to entry followed in the wake of "free" goods, however modest — and they were *very* modest — the size of the public welfare allotments.[16]

Pressure on the Commons

The fear of increased welfare burdens was not the only economic issue confronting established communities every time a stranger sought admission as a resident of some town. In the early years of settlement, each town had considerable land — six to eight miles square, meaning anywhere from 30,000 to 40,000 acres — and relatively few inhabitants. Each resident had legal access to the common pasturage and to any future divisions of land from the huge blocs owned by the town. But as the number of inhabitants increased, and as more and more distributions of town land reduced the available source of unowned land, the per capita supply of land began to shrink. Those inhabitants who had a share in the common pasture and the common lands sought to protect their control over further use and distributions of such property. In town after town, a new rule was imposed: outsiders had to purchase access to rights in the common property from local inhabitants. The result was a new appreciation of private ownership and private control of property, even among men who had grown up in English communities that had used the open field system of farming. The land hunger of New England after 1650 created new incentives to gain and exercise

---

16. On the size of local town charities, see Stephen Foster, *Their Solitary Way: The Puritan Social Ethic in the First Century of Settlement in New England* (New Haven, Connecticut: Yale University Press, 1971), p. 137.

personal sovereignty over the chief economic resource, land.

There was another incentive to reduce the size of the community-owned property: bureaucratic wrangling. Page after page of the Massachusetts town records, year after year: how to restrain access to the common meadow? How to keep midnight visitors from cutting down choice trees for firewood or other uses? How to keep the meadow's fences in repair? Statute followed statute, to no avail. Fines were imposed, equally to no avail. "Free" land meant strong demand for its productivity, and town leaders never were able to find a rational, efficient means of restricting uneconomic uses of the town property. Men had a strong incentive to further their personal economic ends, and far less incentive to consider the public's position. The commons served as incentive to waste, for without a free market and private ownership, it was impossible to calculate accurately the costs and benefits associated with the use of the land. This is the chief economic flaw of all socialist systems, and the early settlers of New England were unable to solve it.

The Continuing Problem of Supply and Demand

Someone who has only a superficial knowledge of the history of the Puritans of the Massachusetts Bay Colony tends to see them as men obsessed with imposing religious restraints or moral restraints on private activities. They were concerned with such questions, as the records indicate, but from the bulk of the legislation, two problems were eternal, unsolvable, and endlessly bothersome to Puritan leaders: 1) pigs without rings in their noses running through the town, and 2) midnight tree cutters on the commons. The tree cutters, like the pigs, insisted on sticking their noses into other people's property.

The commoners — those who had legal access to the common fields and meadows — were too often involved in what today is known as "free riding." They planted crops in the common property, but neglected to keep their portion of the commons properly fenced. It was almost impossible to keep track of who was responsible for which plot. The town had to intervene and assign plots, thus creating opportunities for local political dissension. Animals that wandered around the fenced land often broke down unrepaired fencing between plots, getting into someone else's crops. Tension here was continual.

Fencing inspectors were important officials in every town. Conflicts over responsibility were endless. Without private plots privately repaired, such conflicts were inevitable. In the early decades of Massachusetts, no single public policy prevailed long. First, the colony's General Court — the chief legislative agency — placed the responsibility for fencing on the local town; then it placed the responsibility on the local individual citizen; next it switched back to its original position of town control. The statutes did not function well in practice. Different communities had different problems, and the central government had difficulty in dealing with all of them through the use of any single administrative policy.[17]

The Tragedy of the Commons

The problem facing every selectman in every New England village was the tragedy of the commons, as the biologist Garrett Hardin has called it. Each person who has access to the benefits of public property for use in his own personal business has a positive incentive to drain additional resources from the commons, and he has a very low or even negative incentive to restrain him. The cost of his actions are borne by all the "owners," while the benefits are strictly individual. One more cow or sheep or goat grazing on the town commons will register no noticeable increase in the communally assessed economic burden which rests on any single individual. Yet such grazing is immediately beneficial to the owner of the animal. High benefits, low costs: "Each man is locked into a system that compels him to

---

17. William B. Weeden, *Economic and Social History of New England, 1620-1789,* 2 vols. (New York: Hillary House, [1890] 1963), I, pp. 59-60.

increase his herd without limit—in a world that is limited."[18] It is not surprising that selectmen would find themselves burdened with endless disputes concerning the size of the local herds and the proper—"fair"—assessments of the economic costs of running those herds on the commons.

There is an answer to the tragedy of the commons, at least where it is inexpensive to assign property rights. As C. R. Batten has argued, the transfer of ownership from an amorphous common group to individual citizens provides an incentive to reduce the demands made on the land. Private owners have to assess both costs and benefits of any activity, seeing to it that costs do not outrun benefits.[19] By the end of the seventeenth century, Puritan leaders—or at least leaders who were the descendants of Puritans—reached a similar conclusion.

The Multiplication of Legislation

With each piece of legislation, another set of problems appeared. First, only actual town commoners could run their animals in the common meadow or in the outlying common lands. Only local residents could cut the trees. Later, the selectmen had to impose limits on the number of cattle that could be run, frequently on a "one cow per man" rule. Each man was assessed a few shillings per year for this right. Some people brought in horses; Boston banned them on Sundays. Sheep had to be supervised by a sheep herder. As more animals required full-time supervision, towns hired herdsmen. To keep the cost-per-beast low, each town resident was required by law to run his animal with the herd. Cambridge, for example, imposed a fine of one shilling on anyone whose cow was found on his land after 8 a.m. Since the driver left at 6 a.m., anyone who had not yet delivered his animal to the herd had to escort his cow to the driver, eating

---

18. Hardin, "The Tragedy of the Commons," *Science* (13 Dec., 1968); reprinted in Garrett de Bell (ed.), *The Environmental Handbook* (New York: Ballantine, 1970), p. 37.

19. C. R. Batten, "The Tragedy of the Commons," *The Freeman* (Oct. 1970).

up scarce time. A similar law for goats was passed two years later, in 1639.[20] People naturally attempted to evade the law, and by 1648 the revenues supporting the town's herdsman were not meeting his salary. Consequently, in typical interventionist fashion, the selectmen decided to assess all men a certain amount, whether or not they ran cattle on the commons.[21] A similar rule was established in Watertown in 1665, and the massive evasions encouraged the selectmen to pass an even stiffer law in 1670.[22]

Corrected Over Time

The confusion reigned for decades. As the Watertown records report so eloquently, "there being many complaints made concerning the disorderliness of cattle and swine and the multitudes of sheep in the town, it was voted that the matter above mentioned is left with the selectmen to consider something that may tend to reformation and to present what they shall do to the town to be confirmed."[23] Needless to say, the selectmen could not do anything about it, any more than half a century of Puritan town governments before them. The only solution was the distribution of the commons to local inhabitants — the demise of the commons.

Traditional patterns of life do not die out overnight. Men are usually unwilling to change their way of life unless forced to do so, either by economic circumstances or by direct political pressure. The little town of Sudbury was a case in question. Its inhabitants clung to the old English system of communal property management. The access to the commons was restricted in 1655, and at least thirty younger men received no meadow grants for their animals. They went out of the selectmen's meeting ready to fight. Fight they did, until the town was split. They

---

20. *The Records of the Town of Cambridge, Massachusetts, 1630-1703* (1901), pp. 28, 39.

21. *Ibid.*, p. 72.

22. *Watertown Records* (1894), I, pp. 92, 94-95.

23. *Ibid.*, p. 142.

formed a new community down the road, Marlborough. Not
gaining access to the local commons, they were perfectly willing
to settle for a 24,000-acre plot a few miles away.[24]

Factional strife was not a part of the original goals of the
founders of New England. Factionalism was a blight to be avoided;
this opinion remained a touchstone of American political thought
right down to James Madison's *Federalist #10*. Yet the quarreling
over the commons was incessant, in direct opposition to the
political and communal ideal of the peaceable kingdom.

"Togetherness"

The town of Sudbury was not to be the only Puritan village
unable to cope successfully with the centrifugal forces created
by the presence of socialized property within the town limits.
The creation of Marlborough, despite the fact that the young
founders also established a town commons, testified to the difficulty of preserving both the old common field tenure system and
social peace in the midst of vast stretches of unoccupied land. It
was too easy to move out, and this feature of New England was
to erode the medievalism of early Puritan thought. The central-
ized social control necessary to enforce such a system of common
land required the existence of widespread land scarcity. Ironi-
cally, it was in the final quarter of the seventeenth century that
such land scarcity appeared — scarcity of the most productive
lands — but by that time the haggling over the administration
of the commons and increasing land values had already provided
the incentives necessary to convince both leaders and average
citizens that the commons should be distributed permanently.

One of the original goals of the founders of New England
was that of social cohesion. The life of each community was to
be religiously based. The church was the center of the town, both
symbolically and very often physically. Men were to live close
to each other, share in each other's burdens, pray together, and
construct God's kingdom on earth. But there was a strong eco-

---

24. Powell, *Puritan Village*, ch. 9.

nomic incentive to consolidate land holdings.

Even before the market of Boston created demand for agricultural products, men in the villages had begun to barter their land allotments. A man might live in the town with five or six acres of garden and meadow, and he might also have been given some forty or fifty-acre plots in the common lands scattered around the town. Obviously, it was to the advantage of some men to consolidate their holdings, trading with others who also wanted to cut down on the time spent to travel – in mud, in snow, in dust – from one plot to another. Then, family by family, an exodus began from the central town. Artisans tended to come into the town's center; farmers, especially those affected by Boston's market (those in the immediate Boston area or close to water transport to Boston), needed to consolidate in order to rationalize production.

Despite the efforts of ministers and local selectmen, the population spread out; decentralization, when not political, was at least social. You could not examine your neighbor's intimate affairs when he was three miles away. The market for land was an agent of social decentralization.

The Urge for Private Ownership

The experience of the isolated little town of Dedham is illustrative of the effect of market freedom on traditional patterns of social and economic control. Professor Kenneth Lockridge describes the process:

If the corporate unity of the village was slowly eroding, so was its physical coherence. The common field system began disintegrating almost from the day of its inception. Already in the 1640's the town permitted men to "fence their lots in particular" and presumably to grow in these lots whichever crops they wished. By the 1670's it had become usual for men to take up both special "convenience grants" and their usual shares of each new dividend in locations as close as possible to their existing lots, practices which aided the consolidation of individual holdings. The process encouraged by public policy was completed by private transactions, for an active market in small parcels soon emerged, a market in which most farmers sought to sell distant lands and buy lands closer to their main holdings. The new result was the coalescence of private farms. From here, it would be but two short steps for farmers whose holdings were centered in outlying areas to move their barns and then their houses from the village out to their lands. As of 1686 few seem to have taken these steps, but the way had been prepared and the days of a society totally enclosed by the village were numbered. In any event the common-field system was gone, taking with it the common decisions and the frequent encounters of every farmer with his fellows which it entailed.[25]

The closer to Boston, the faster these changes occurred, for with transport cheap enough — within 10 miles or so along a well-traveled road — the effects of the free market could be felt far more alluringly. It paid to become more efficient.

Cambridge lay across the Charles River from Boston. The demise of the commons in Cambridge seems typical. The first division took place in 1662. A second followed in 1665. Two small divisions were made in 1707 and 1724. Various methods were used to determine who got what parcels of land: lots were drawn, or acres were distributed in terms of the number of cows a family was allowed to graze on the common meadow, or a committee was formed to consider other methods. In some towns there was considerable strife; in others, the distributions were relatively peaceful. The effects on Cambridge were significant, and in retrospect they seem quite predictable. After 1691, it was no longer necessary to pass new laws against the cutting of timber from the commons. Men owned their own land, and they cut or refused to cut as they saw fit. It was no longer necessary to pass laws against selling timber to men from other towns, a common feature of mid-seventeenth century legislation in the towns. A thoroughly individualistic system of land tenure evolved.

Opposition to the Andros Regime

The final impetus to private ownership came in the 1680's.

---

25. Kenneth Lockridge, *A New England Town: The First Hundred Years — Dedham, Massachusetts, 1636-1736* (New York: Norton, 1970), p. 82.

James II, after coming to the throne in 1685, sent Sir Edmund Andros, the former royal governor of New York, to take over as governor general of New England. The king meant to consolidate the political structure of the colonies, making them all purely royal colonies. Andros met with instant opposition. He began to hit too close to a crucial legal weakness of New England's towns.

By 1685, there were four New England colonies, New Haven having been absorbed into Connecticut in 1662: Massachusetts, Plymouth, Connecticut, and Rhode Island. (Plymouth became a part of Massachusetts in 1692.) The right of these colonial governments to create valid, legal townships was in question; the right of the towns to act as if they were incorporated entities in giving legal title to land was not in doubt: it was illegal. The king's seal was not present in the towns, and this was an invitation for the king's newly appointed bureaucracy — a growing horde — to intervene to their own advantage.

In 1686, the Andros regime imposed a 2.5 shilling quit-rent per annum on all 100-acre lots not occupied or occupied by means of defective titles. Andros called for a re-examination of the land patents. Whether or not this represented a true threat to the majority of land owners, they certainly were convinced that his intentions were the worst and that a major land-grab was about to be inaugurated. In the various political pamphlets issued in 1688-90 by outraged critics of his administration (later assembled as the *Andros Tracts*), this criticism was made over and over. It was a major reason cited as a justification for his overthrow in 1688. "Henceforward, the colonies took absolute control of the land. . . ."[26] Men desired, as never before, to gain clear-cut title to their lands. It intensified a pressure that was five decades or more old.[27]

---

26. Roy H. Akagi, *The Town Proprietors of the New England Colonies* (Gloucester, Massachusetts: Peter Smith, [1924] 1963), p. 124.

27. Philip J. Greven, *Four Generations: Population, Land, and Family in Colonial Andover, Massachusetts* (Ithaca, New York: Cornell University Press, 1970), p. 61.

Conclusion

Step by step, individual men asserted their sovereignty over land; the proprietors of the commons steadily transferred the unoccupied land surrounding the village, as well as the land in the more central common fields, to the citizens of the town. While they did not ask for competitive bidding as a means of distributing this land, the officials did effect a continuous transformation of ownership. In doing so, they established a break from the historical inheritance of many towns, the old medieval open field system of common ownership. The continual bickering over the allocation of timber, fallen logs, tree cutting by moonlight, town herds, herdsmen's salaries, fence mending, planting in the common fields, and policing everyone to see that these laws were obeyed, finally broke the will of the town officials. It was easier to give the land away; it was also more profitable for town residents, in most cases.

The tradition of the independent yeoman farmer so impressed Jefferson that he built an entire political philosophy around it. The idea that individual men are more responsible for the administration of property than boards of political appointees or even elected officials became a fundamental principle of eighteenth and nineteenth century American life. The concepts of personal responsibility and personal authority became interlocked, and the great symbol of this fusion was the family farm. The endless quest for land by American families is one of the most impressive tales in American history. It began as soon as the Pilgrims stepped off the *Mayflower* and their Puritan neighbors stepped off the *Arabella* a decade later. The experiment in common ownership in village after village over half a century convinced ministers, laymen, and political leaders that the private ownership of the means of production was not only the most efficient way to get Christian goals accomplished, but also that such a form of ownership was economically profitable as well. They saw, almost from the start, that *social peace is best achieved by means of the private ownership of the tools of production, especially that most crucial of tools, land.* This lesson of that first half-century of New England Puritan life is one of the most important heritages of American life. Without it, indeed, American life would be impossible to interpret correctly.

2

PRICE CONTROLS

The court having found by experience, that it would not avail by any law to redress the excessive rates of laborers' and workmen's wages, etc. (for being restrained, they would either remove to other places where they might have more, or else being able to live by planting and other employments of their own, they would not be hired at all), it was therefore referred to the several towns to set the rates among themselves. This took better effect, so that in a voluntary way, by the counsel and persuasion of the elders, and example of some who led the way, they were brought to more moderation than they could be by compulsion. But it held not long.

Gov. John Winthrop [1]

The little band of Pilgrims who settled Plymouth Colony in 1620 are more famous in children's textbooks than their neighbors, the Puritans. Plymouth Rock, Thanksgiving, Miles Standish, and Speaking for Yourself, John, are all ingrained in the story of America's origin. Nevertheless, in terms of historical impact, the Pilgrims never rivaled their Puritan neighbors. Plymouth Colony remained a relatively isolated and closed society until it finally merged with Massachusetts in 1692. It was Gov. John Winthrop, not Gov. William Bradford, who left his mark on American institutions.

---

1. James K. Hosmer (ed.), *Winthrop's Journal: "History of New England," 1630-1649*, 2 vols. (New York: Barnes & Noble, [1908] 1966), II, p. 24.

The first generation of New Englanders were an optimistic bunch. Even those social and religious outcasts who wound up in Rhode Island shared this faith in the future. The Puritans, in the famous words of Gov. Winthrop, expected to become a "city on a hill," like the shining community mentioned in the Gospel of Matthew (5:14) — a light to the darkness of the world, an example of how godly living, both personal and social, might bring prosperity and peace on earth.[2] By the preaching of the gospel and the establishment of Christian institutions, they believed, Christian reconstruction of the world is not only possible but mandatory.[3] This vision is best seen in the history of New England written by Edward Johnson in 1653: "I am now pressed for the service of our God Christ, to re-build the most glorious Edifice of Mount Zion in a wilderness. . . . Then my dear friend unfold thy hands, for thou and I have much work to do, aye, and all Christian Soldiers in the world throughout."[4]

The question of what constituted a truly godly economic system did not immediately disturb them. The leaders of the colony were sons of the lesser British gentry, made up of men trained in law, theology, and the classical education of the universities, Cambridge and Oxford. Most of the people were farmers, with a scattering of craftsmen and artisans (too few, as they were to discover); they were literate, reflecting the Puritan emphasis on education, but hardly scholars. What little economics their leaders brought with them was basically the economics of the medieval schoolmen. Economics was only just beginning to become an independent discipline in England; there were no

---

2. John Winthrop, "A Modell of Christian Charity" (1630), in Edmund S. Morgan (ed.), *The Founding of Massachusetts: Historians and the Sources* (New York: Bobbs-Merrill, 1964), pp. 190-204.

3. On the optimism of the first generation of Puritans in New England, see Aletha Joy Gilsdorf, "The Puritan Apocalypse: New England Eschatology in the Seventeenth Century" (Ph.D. dissertation, history, Yale University, 1966), esp. pp. 119-20. See also Iain Murray, *The Puritan Hope* (London: Banner of Truth, 1971).

4. J. Franklin Jameson (ed.), *Johnson's Wonder-Working Providence, 1628-1651* (New York: Barnes & Noble, [1910] 1952), p. 52.

professional academic economists, and very few men were more than pamphleteers, even among the "professionals." Thus, it is not surprising that the first two generations of leaders in New England should have fallen back upon "tried and true" medieval economic concepts. One of these was the concept of the just price.

A "Just" Price

A lot of needless confusion has emerged from discussions of scholars concerning the just price. From the time of Thomas Aquinas right up until the mid-seventeenth century, a "just" price was assumed to be the market price during "normal" times. No widely read schoolman ever tried to compute some mathematically precise formula on the basis of ethics; indeed, Aquinas himself had denied that such precision is possible.[5] The problem of justice arose when there were disruptions in the market—a war, a famine, a local production monopoly—that made it appear that justice was being thwarted by greedy exploiters. Then the standard approach was to assemble a group of distinguished, "impartial" leaders in the community, and they were supposed to determine the proper prices for various commodities. The goal, officially, was consumer protection. More often the result was the creation of an even more monopolistic guild, for the "just" or "reasonable" price was, in the absence of a competitive market price, computed on a "cost-plus" basis. As in World War II, this was more apt to lead to producer protection—from more competitive producers.[6]

These restrictions on free entry—to guarantee "quality" production from "unscrupulous" producers who would offer shoddy goods at lower prices—were the foundation of the medieval guild system. Similar restrictions operated in New

---

5. Thomas Aquinas, *Summa Theologica, II-II*, Quest. 77.

6. Price competition broadens the scope of the market by making goods and services available to buyers formerly too poor to enter the market. It was the fundamental form of competition in the coming of modern capitalism: Max Weber, *General Economic History* (New York: Collier [1920] 1961), p. 230.

England during the first half-century of its existence. Licensing, municipality-enforced inspections, and self-policing by guild members were all features of the medieval city and the New England town. But the most common feature was a system of price and wage controls.

Early Controls

Almost from the beginning, the colony of the Massachusetts Bay Company placed controls on the wages of artisans. The colony was begun in 1629; in 1630 a law was passed which established wage ceilings for carpenters, joiners, bricklayers, sawyers, and thatchers.[7] Common laborers were limited to twelve shillings a day, or six if meat and drink were provided by the employer. Any artisan violating this statute was to be assessed a ten shilling fine. The effect of these wage ceilings must have presented itself almost immediately: an excess of demand for the services of artisans over the available supply. Under such conditions, it is always difficult to recruit labor. Within six months, these wage ceilings were repealed, leaving wages "free and at liberty as men shall reasonable agree."[8] The implication was clear enough, however: if men should again grow unreasonable, the controls would be reimposed. They were.

The history of price and wage controls in New England is an "on again, off again" affair. The year 1633 brought a new set of regulations, a law which the magistrates saw fit to repeal in 1635.[9] The repeal was of a special nature, however. The civil government imposed a general profit margin of 33 percent on any goods sold retail in the colonies if the particular good was imported. No imported good could therefore be sold for over 33 percent above the London price.[10] The magistrates then inserted

---

7. Nathaniel B. Shurtleff (ed.), *Records of the Governor and Company of the Massachusetts Bay in New England*, 5 vols. (Boston: William White, Commonwealth Printer, 1853), I, p. 74. [Cited hereafter as *Mass. Col. Recs.*]

8. *Ibid.*, I, p. 84.

9. *Ibid.*, I, pp. 104, 159-60.

10. *Ibid.*, I, pp. 159-60: the maximum rate was 4d/s, that is, 4 pence per shilling, or 4/12, or 33 percent.

a clause which was almost calculated to drive merchants and laborers to distraction. Instead of setting forth in the statute a precise, predictable definition of what constitutes economic injustice, and therefore a breach of the written law, the magistrates chose instead to warn citizens against violating the *intent* of the law:

> Whereas the former laws, the one concerning the wages of workmen, the other concerning the prices of commodities, were for diverse good considerations repealed, this present Court, now, for avoiding such mischiefs as may follow thereupon by such ill-disposed persons as may take liberty to oppress and wrong their neighbors, by taking excessive wages for work, or unreasonable prices for such necessary merchandise or other commodities as shall pass from man to man, it is therefore now ordered, that if any man shall offend in any of the said cases against the true intent of this law, he shall be punished by fine or imprisonment, according to the quality of the offense, as the Court upon lawful trial and conviction shall adjudge.[11]

In short, there was a law against "excess profits" back in 1635, and it provided the law enforcement agents with a considerably broad unspecified coverage. The men involved in trade in 1635 had about as little notion of what constituted the limits of state authority in the realm of economics as men have today. The 33 percent figure was one of the few to appear in the legislation of that era, but men could never be certain that the court or courts would uphold the validity of any given transaction. It made for a considerable degree of uncertainty in economic exchange.

The Road to Serfdom

Max Weber, the great German sociologist, argued on several occasions that the essence of both theocratic commonwealths and socialist regimes is this reliance upon substantive concepts of justice. The law of the land is governed in terms of a higher ethical or theological system than mere economic efficiency or

---

11. *Ibid.*, I, p. 160.

the possibilities for profit. (It could be argued, of course, that the emphasis on economic efficiency to the exclusion of everything else is equally religious in impact, equally ethical.) What characterizes most capitalist economies, on the other hand, is a system of written, formal, predictable law that inhibits the decision-making power of theocratic rulers or socialist bureaucrats and planners. F. A. Hayek concurs with Weber, and his *Road to Serfdom*[12] and especially *The Constitution of Liberty*[13] are eloquent defenses of the rule of formal law as the foundation of the free society as well as the free market. What is essential to capitalism, both Hayek and Weber agree, is *legal predictability*. Written law is important, though not absolutely essential. England, for example, has resisted a formal written constitution for centuries, while the Soviet Union has a nicely written constitution that is operationally impotent. Men need to know what to expect from the civil government if they are to plan rationally and make economic decisions effectively.

The magistrates, by assuming that the inherited medieval concern about "ethical" pricing was the Christian approach to economic affairs, necessarily created a dilemma for themselves and the citizens of Massachusetts. How does one determine what is a just price? What are the legitimate limits on economic oppression? How is the individual bargainer to estimate whether or not he is making an infraction against the "true intent of this law"? What are the legitimate limits on state authority? Prediction becomes exceedingly difficult, for the traders can never be sure of how the magistrates — who were also the final court of appeals — would estimate "the quality of the offense."

Another problem was the establishment of the locus of authority. Should the local civil government set prices in terms of local conditions, or is the central government responsible? In October, 1636, the General Court of Massachusetts delegated the author-

---

12. Hayek, *The Road to Serfdom* (Chicago: University of Chicago Press, 1944).

13. Hayek, *The Constitution of Liberty* (Chicago: University of Chicago Press, 1960).

ity to regulate prices and wages to the various towns.[14] Neverthe-less, the magistrates could not resist the cry of "oppression," and in March of 1638, a committee was set up to investigate com-plaints against exorbitant prices and wages. Such ruthless pric-ing, the authorities state, is "to the great dishonor of God, the scandal of the gospel, and the grief of diverse of God's people, both here in this land and in the land of our maturity. . . ."[15] The city on a hill was not setting a godly example to the heathen and the people back home in England. The central government continued to maintain its right to step in and regulate prices when such action seemed warranted by the situation, but in general the towns did most of the regulating work after 1636. Only with the great Indian war of 1675-76 did the central government step in to take vigorous action against high prices. As Prof. Richard B. Morris summarizes the history of the con-trols: "The codes of 1648 and 1660, and the supplement of 1672, continued substantially the basic law of 1636 against oppression in wages and prices, leaving to the freemen of each town the authority to settle the rates of pay."[16]

Connecticut's Wage Code

The other Puritan colonies were no better, with the exception of the Pilgrim group in Plymouth. Connecticut's General Court insisted that men had not proved reliable when left as "a law unto themselves," and therefore it passed an incredibly detailed wage code. At first, the officials apparently had no insight into the consequences of the regulatory nightmare they were con-structing. Skilled craftsmen were not to accept more than 20 pence a day (12 pence to a shilling) from March 10 through October 11, nor above 18 pence for work on any other day during the year. This included carpenters, masons, coopers, smiths, and

---

14. *Mass. Col. Recs.*, I, p. 183.

15. *Ibid.*, I, p. 223.

16. Richard B. Morris, *Government and Labor in Early America* (New York: Colum-bia University Press, 1941), p. 62.

wheelwrights. All other handicraft workers were prohibited from taking more than 18 pence per day for the first half of the year, nor more than 12 pence during the remainder of the year. Workers were obligated to work an eleven-hour day in the summer, in addition to eating and sleeping, and nine hours in the winter. Price controls were placed on sawed boards.[17] This jumbled mass of legislation was repealed within a decade.[18]

New Haven Colony, which was merged with Connecticut in 1662, imposed controls in 1640, just as the great economic depression of the 1640's struck New England.[19] No longer would there be the massive exodus of Puritans from England, for the Civil War of the Cromwell era had begun, and English Puritans stayed in the British Isles to fight. Thus, the capital and currency brought in by immigrants from 1630-40 was instantly cut off. Prices collapsed almost overnight. The irony of imposing price controls in the year of the beginning of a collapse in prices should be obvious. As in the comparable medieval legislation, a group of supposedly disinterested men served as the committee which judged individual situations in cases involving disputes.[20] These controls do not appear in the 1656 law code of the colony, indicating that they had abandoned price controls in the intervening period.

The Trial of Captain Keayne, an Untypical Case

Historians are not agreed on the actual effects of such legislation. Some think that the Puritans were in dead earnest about enforcing the codes.[21] On the other hand, one scholar has argued that they probably were not that crucial in operation; between

---

17. J. Hammond Trumball and Charles Hoadly (eds.), *The Public Records of the Colony of Connecticut*, 15 vols. (New York: A.M.S. Press, [1850-90] 1968), I, (1641), p. 65. [Cited hereafter as *Conn. Col. Recs.*]

18. *Ibid.*, I, (1650), p. 205.

19. Charles Hoadly (ed.), *Records of the Colony and Plantation of New Haven 1630-1649* (Hartford: for the editor, 1857), pp. 35-36, 52, 55.

20. *Ibid.*, p. 55.

21. Morris, *Government & Labor*, p. 72.

1630 and 1644 — the years of the most rigorous legislation in Massachusetts Bay Colony — less than twenty people were actually convicted for violating the wage and price guidelines. Twice as many people were convicted for speaking out against public authority in this period.[22] The most famous case was the trial of Capt. Robert Keayne, but there is good reason not to regard this as a typical case.

Capt. Keayne, officer of the Artillery Company, was a zealous Puritan, a merchant of Boston, a public leader, and the subject of the most famous economic trials of New England. The 1639 trial involved a dispute over his alleged price gouging; the 1642 trial involved a dispute with a local woman over the ownership of a sow. (Incredibly, this was one of the most important trials in American history. The dispute over its result — Keayne was judged innocent by the magistrates — led to the establishment of a bicameral legislature, for the elected representatives of the towns, the deputies, sided with Keayne's opponent, goodwife (Goodie) Sherman. The magistrates had vetoed the deputies, and the deputies finally pressed for a division in the legislature. A pig helped to destroy unicameralism in America!)[23] In the 1639 trial, Keayne was convicted of economic oppression, and he was fined 200 pounds (later reduced to 80 pounds by the magistrates, to the dismay of the more "democratic" deputies), and he was forced to confess his economic sins before the First Church in Boston. This is the only case of economic confession in the archives of the Massachusetts ecclesiastical records.[24] Thus, far from being typical, this famous trial was more of a pre-1640 symbol. Once his "deviant" behavior was exposed

---

22. Marrion H. Gottfried, "The First Depression in Massachusetts," *New England Quarterly*, XI (1936), p. 640.

23. T. H. Breen, *The Character of the Good Ruler* (New Haven, Connecticut: Yale University Press, 1970), p. 79. The debate raged for two years, 1642-44. The split occurred in 1644.

24. Emil Oberholzer, *Delinquent Saints* (New York: Columbia University Press, 1956), p. 189.

publicly, the public promptly forgot about it, although Keayne never did.

Keayne's Self-Defense

Keayne's last will and testament, which has become one of the most important of all primary source documents for early New England history, records his disapproval of the whole affair. He desperately wanted to clear his name, a decade and a half later, even to the point of asking his estate's overseers to petition the General Court to repeal the original sentence "and to return my find again after all this time of enjoying it . . . which I believe is properly due to my estate and will not be comfortable for the country to enjoy."[25] His economic practices had been fair, he claimed, and well within the bounds of merchants' ethics. Those who had accused him were all liars, he said, and he spent several pages of his will to refute them. Furthermore, other men had committed really serious crimes, but they had been fined lightly. Keayne's most incisive observation related to the changed status of some of his former detractors. This statement offers considerable insight into the process of gradual decontrol of the economy after 1650:

[My own offense] was so greatly aggravated and with such indignation pursued by some, as if no censure could be too great or too severe, as if I had not been worthy to have lived upon the earth. [Such offenses] are not only now common almost in every shop and warehouse but even then and ever since with a higher measure of excess, yea even by some of them that were most zealous and had their hands and tongues deepest in my censure. [At that time] they were buyers, [but since then] they are turned sellers and peddling merchants themselves, so that they [the crimes] are become no offenses now nor are worthy questioning nor taking notice of in others.[26]

What had taken place to change the public's opinion about

---

25. Bernard Bailyn (ed.), *The Apologia of Robert Keayne* (New York: Harper Torchbook, 1964), p. 51.

26. *Ibid.*, p. 48.

price controls? First, as Keayne noted, the self-interest of some of the participants had changed, as their ethics had changed. Second, the depression of 1640-45 had begun to slacken in the later 1640's, and one of the sources of revival was the birth of the New England shipping trade. The merchants were important in the economy now — crucial, in fact — and their influence could not be ignored without cost. New England in 1650 was no hotbed of laissez-faire capitalism by any stretch of the imagination (or manipulation of the footnotes), but the old suspicion toward business was never completely revived after the 1640's.

A Problem for Politicians

Keayne's case had posed a serious problem for the political leaders and the ministers who served as their advisers. (Ministers were not permitted to hold political office in New England, for this was regarded as a breach of separation between two God-ordained offices. There was no separation of Christianity and state — except, as always, among the outcasts of Rhode Island — but there was an official separation of powers, sword and word.) Gov. John Winthrop records in his diary the problems confronting the judges. Rev. John Cotton, probably the leading social theorist among the New England clergy, had outlined for the magistrates the standard medieval critique of free pricing, already over four centuries old in European thought. First, no man has the right to buy as cheaply as he can in all cases, nor sell as dearly as he can in all cases, even if the market should permit it. Second, no man of business should take advantage of another's ignorance to make a profit. Third, he may not sell above the current market price, even to make up for losses on other items, a restriction which was basic to medieval Christian casuistry. (Casuistry: the application of general principles to specific circumstances.)

In applying these standards in Keayne's case, Winthrop said, the magistrates had tended toward leniency. He offered several reasons why. First, there was no law prohibiting profit as such. Second, because men in all countries use their advantage to raise retail prices. Third, he was not alone in his fault. But the fundamental point was the final one. It is here that we see the ultimate chink in the armor of all price control schemes, from A. D. 1100 to the present: "Because a certain rule could not be found out for an equal rate between buyer and seller, though much labor had been bestowed upon it, and diverse laws had been made, which, upon experience, were repealed, as being neither safe nor equal."[27] Aquinas himself had warned that "the just price of things is not fixed with mathematical precision, but depends on a kind of estimate, so that a slight addition or subtraction would not seem to destroy the equality of justice."[28] Finding that elusive "equal rate" proved to be more of a task than successive pieces of legislation could achieve in New England, no less than in Europe as a whole. No one knew what a just price was.

Kai Erikson has written with respect to social deviants that they perform a kind of communal function. The deviant is ushered into his role "by a decisive and often dramatic ceremony, yet is retired from it with scarcely a word of public notice."[29] This was certainly Keayne's fate. He was later elected as a magistrate, and his occasional lapses into drunkenness are noted in the official records only by the imposition of small fines. The humiliation of the trial disturbed him until his dying day, but the Puritan community, having made its point, was content to let bygones be bygones. It had asserted its medieval economic standards, and it promptly went about undermining them, a fact which Keayne saw clearly, but which did not bother the majority of his more energetic contemporaries. So long as a man's conscience was sound and his intent was just, he was free to go about his business. Obviously, to prove the state of a man's conscience, especially if the suspect happened to be a leader in Puritan politics, industry, or shipping, would be no easy task. This

---

27. *Winthrop's Journal*, I, p. 316.

28. Aquinas, *Summa Theologica*, II-II, Quest. 77.

29. Kai T. Erikson, *Wayward Puritans* (New York: Wiley, 1966), p. 16.

difficulty would be far more obvious to the magistrates in 1650 than it had been in 1639.

Wage Controls in 1641

The last major attempt by the central government of Massachusetts to control wages in peacetime came in 1641. The scarcity of money — scarce in comparison to prices common the year before — had disrupted the economic life of New England. Immigration from England came to a standstill; indeed, a few energetic Puritans returned to England to participate in the Civil War against Charles I. Merchants were closing their doors, and manufacturers were refusing to hire laborers. The General Court declared that laborers must accept a mandatory reduction of wages proportional to the reduced price of the particular commodity they labored to make. Laborers, the law declared, "are to be content to partake now in the present scarcity, as well as they had their advantage in the plenty of former times. . . ."[30] At least the magistrates had enough sense to control prices in the general direction of the market. In tying the laborer's wage to the value of his output, they acknowledged the close relation between the market price of the produced good and the value of labor's services. In contrast to modern wage controls during a depression — wage floors, compulsory collective bargaining, artificial restrictions on entry into labor markets, and so forth — the Puritans of 1641 understood that laborers should accept a lower wage if the value of their output was falling. Three centuries later, their descendants were not to show equal wisdom in the face of a similar collapse in price expectations, even those who were the officially certified experts in economics, a discipline undreamed of in 1641. The Puritans used shipping and increased agricultural output to revive their economy; their descendants used deficit financing and a world war, and even then their

---

30. *Mass. Col. Recs.*, I, p. 326.

depression lasted longer.[31] The price controls of the seventeenth century, however misguided, were a lot more sensible than those of the twentieth century.

1675-76: The Turning Point

After 1650, there was a relaxation of economic controls, especially price controls. (The controls on product quality and guild output did continue, sporadically.) As the new shipping trade expanded, the market expanded. This expansion of market transactions, especially in the Boston vicinity, encouraged the greater specialization of production, and hence encouraged greater economic productivity. Furthermore, as more people entered the markets, both as producers and buyers, the ability of individuals to manipulate specific prices decreased. There was more competition, greater knowledge concerning alternative prices and substitutes, and more familiarity with trade. The price spread between producer and consumer naturally decreased as participants became more skilled in their transactions. Thus, the need for specific legislation was reduced, as far as the magistrates were concerned. Medieval just-price theory had always accepted market pricing as valid, except in "uncommon" or emergency conditions, and with the expansion of the free market came a respite from political intervention into market pricing. The last great outburst of intervention came in 1675-76, during the serious Indian uprising known as King Philip's War.[32] (At almost exactly the same time, Virginia also suffered a major Indian uprising.)[33]

People seldom hear of King Philip's War today, yet in terms of the percentage of Americans who died in any war, this was

---

31. The colonies did impose various kinds of trade restrictions, including embargoes, government monopsonies, and so forth, which undoubtedly prolonged the depression.

32. Douglas E. Leach, *Flintlock and Tomahawk: New England in King Philip's War* (New York: Norton, 1966).

33. Wilcomb E. Washburn, *The Governor and the Rebel: A History of Bacon's Rebellion in Virginia* (Chapel Hill: University of North Carolina Press, 1957), ch. 2.

by far the worst. The Indians, led by their prince who was known as King Philip by the whites, struck without warning up and down the edge of the New England frontier. For almost a year it looked as though they would triumph, or at least seriously restrict European settlement in the area. Estimates of the loss of life have ranged above ten percent of the total population of the whites, unmatched by any other U.S. war. Thousands lost their homes and fled to the urban areas of more populated towns. Understandably, such population shifts put terrible burdens on the New England economy. Outfitting the militia and paying the salaries intensified the disruption, as men left their farms and shops to join the armed forces.

Pastoral Pessimism

For years, Puritan preaching had become increasingly pessimistic in approach. After 1660, the old theological optimism had begun to fade, and a new sermon style appeared. Known today as the "jeremiad," these sermons warned the people against the consequences of sin and the failure of the young generation to join the churches as members (membership had always been a minority affair in New England, but after 1660 it was even more of a minority affair). Michael Wigglesworth's famous poem, the *Day of Doom*,[34] and his less famous *God's Controversy with New England*,[35] became best-sellers in their day (the early 1660's). Pastors warned of God's impending judgment; the old faith in New England as a triumphant "city on a hill" appeared less and less in their sermons. The Indian uprising seemed to confirm all the dire prophecies of the ministers.

Rev. Increase Mather (who along with his son Cotton became the most prolific writing team in American history) pressed the General Court to pass a list of "Provoking Evils" that had brought on the curse of the war. The "democratic" deputies

---

34. Reprinted in Harrison T. Meserole (ed.), *Seventeenth-Century American Poetry* (Garden City, New York: Doubleday, 1968), pp. 42-54.

35. *Ibid.*, pp. 55-113.

instantly followed his advice; the "aristocratic" magistrates held out for a week, until the news of another Indian victory forced them into action. The list included the usual social failings: the ignoring of God's warnings, the many uncatechized children in the commonwealth, the decline of church membership, the wearing of wigs, long hair among men, luxurious wardrobes, and the existence of Quakers (this issue had faded in the early 1650's). (Topless fashions among women – far more common in 1675 than today – drew a fine of 90 percent less than the fine for being a Quaker, which may indicate something about Puritan priorities in 1675.) But the list of "Provoking Evils" could not be rounded out without calling attention to various economic oppressions. Double restitution for price gouging was imposed (for the amount of the overcharge); fines could also be imposed by the court. (Today, we also hear suggestions to impose a system of restitution for crime victims, but with this grim variation: the victims are to be reimbursed by the taxpayers, not the criminals.[36]) Complaints against artisans and merchants could be lodged by "victims," but there was no mention of inflated agricultural prices.[37]

The key concern of the magistrates was shown in the following year, 1676. Inhabitants of different counties were charging varying prices for the same goods sold to the militia. (You can be virtually assured that the higher prices appeared in those areas where the militia was actively engaged at any point in time.) The General Court asserted that goods and services are the same in value, wherever found, that is, a rifle is a rifle in any county of Massachusetts. The answer to this problem, said the Court, was the imposition of full-scale price controls, and this became law on May 3, 1676. This was the last fling; not for another century, when a new war broke out, would any New England legislature pass such a comprehensive scheme of price controls. So they created a central council:

36. Cf. *Trial* (May/June, 1972), the publication of the American Trial Lawyers Association.

37. *Mass. Col. Recs.*, V, pp. 59ff.

It is ordered by this Court, that a committee shall be chosen in each county to examine the rates put upon all manner of things used or expended for the public, and to view the particular bills allowed by the militia of each town for expenses, until the first of this instant [month]. And so far as they judge right and equal, to pass the same under their hands. And the committees abovesaid are hereby ordered to choose one man from among themselves, in every [one] of the counties, who shall meet at Boston the first fourth day in July next, and bring with them the accounts allowed and passed in the several counties, where and when their work shall be to compare them together, and to regulate the whole, as to them shall seem most just and equal. . . .[38]

One Last Try; Then, Capitulation

A very similar piece of legislation was passed by the Connecticut legislature in the same month.[39] Under the pressure of war, the magistrates and deputies could not resist the lure of officially stable, universal prices. The lessons provided by four and a half decades of price control legislation had not sunk in; the leaders still thought that they could legislate away the economic realities of scarcity and dislocation. Fortunately for the New England economy, the war ended before the year was over; the price controls of 1676 were allowed to lapse before the shortages, black markets, and disrupted supplies that are the inevitable products of price controls could appear.

This was the high-water mark for price controls in New England. English mercantilism imposed controls on external trade, but not until 1776 were the people of New England to see full-scale price and wage controls. (Those controls proved to be economically disastrous.[40]) After 1676, a whole series of restraints on free bargaining were allowed to fade away. Controls on fashion — status-oriented sumptuary laws — disappeared. As

---

38. *Ibid.*, V, p. 79.

39. *Conn. Col. Recs.*, V, pp. iv-v.

40. Percy Greaves, "From Price Control to Valley Forge, 1777-1778," *The Freeman* (Feb. 1972).

I discussed in Chapter One, controls on the buying and selling of land were abandoned. Clearly, it was the end of an era. A half-century of experimentation with intermittent price and wage controls had ended.

There was one exception to this general rule. The Massachusetts legislature did try, from time to time, to regulate the price and quality of bread. This continued until 1720. Finally, the legislature passed one last bill, an incredibly complex set of regulations on the price and size of each loaf—four general price categories, 23 different weights, three types (white, wheaton, household) — and explained why such a law was necessary. The preface of this bill is an archetypal summary of the total ineffectiveness of price controls through the ages:

> . . . the act made and passed in the eighth year of King William III, entitled "an act for the due assize of bread," is found not effectual for the good ends and purposes therein designed, and a little or no observance has been made thereof, but covetous and evil-disposed persons have, for their own gain, deceived and oppressed his majesty's subjects, more especially the poorer sort. . . .[41]

I have not been able to ascertain if anyone was ever brought to trial as a result of this law, but there is no indication in the colony records that I have been able to locate that this control of bread prices was ever attempted again. My guess is that this absence is not due to the success of the law in thwarting "covetous and evil-disposed persons," but rather the law was, as all the others before it had been, a failure. The search for the "just price" was over.

Conclusion

The Puritans had to be a practical people. The New England wilderness was a rugged testing ground. Commitment to principle was important for their religious and psychological survival, but they were always convinced that Christianity is an eminently

---

41. *Acts and Resolves of the Province of Massachusetts Bay*, 21 vols. (Boston: State Printer, 1869), II, p. 166.

practical religion. If a particular policy failed again and again, then Puritan political leaders and ministers were willing to re-think the policy. Either it had to be based on a false principle or else there had to be a misapplication of a general principle. After half a century of failure with price control legislation, Puritans were quite willing to let the civil government retreat from the market's pricing activities. They did not stop preaching about economic oppression or personal immorality in economic trans-actions, but they no longer sought to involve the machinery of civil government in questions of cost and price.

The important fact for American economic history is that the old belief, imported uncritically in the name of Christianity, that the civil government needs to set "just" prices, was abandoned. A medieval legacy — itself the product more of Aristotelian logic than biblical exposition — no longer was assumed to be neces-sary in a Christian commonwealth. Men were left free to truck and barter at prices determined by mutual consent. A crucial break with an intellectual tradition that had been somewhat hostile to the free market was accomplished in 1676. Americans in peacetime would be left free to pursue their vocations as they chose, not as some governmental panel of "disinterested, distin-guished persons" might choose.

3

SUMPTUARY LEGISLATION

. . . we cannot but account it our duty to commend unto all sorts of persons a sober and moderate use of those blessings which, beyond our expectation, the LORD has been pleased to afford unto us in this wilderness, and also declare our utter detestation and dislike that men or women of mean condition, educations, and callings should take upon them the garb of gentlemen, by the wearing of gold or silver lace, or buttons, or points at their knees, to walk in great boots; or women of the same rank to wear tiffany hoods or scarves, which though allowable to persons of greater estates, or more liberal education, yet we cannot but judge it intolerable in persons of such like condition. . . .[1]

Sumptuary laws, as defined by one dictionary, are "laws regulating extravagance in food, dress, etc. on religious or moral grounds." No other aspect of Puritan social legislation during the first half century of New England life better testifies to the fundamentally medieval orientation of that culture. Yet the grandsons of these men became the Yankees — the sharp traders, mobile entrepreneurs, and practical inventors whose outlook on life was that of Ben Franklin's creation, *Poor Richard's Almanack.*

---

1. Nathaniel B. Shurtleff (ed.), *Records of the Governor and Company of the Massachusetts Bay in New England*, 5 vols. (Boston: State Printer, 1853), III, p. 243. I have cited the version approved by the more democratic deputies; the version approved by the full General Court is almost identical: *ibid*, IV, pt. I, pp. 61-62. [Cited hereafter as *Mass. Col. Recs.*]

This astounding transformation from Puritan to Yankee has fascinated historians for many years, and the fate of the sumptuary legislation serves as a kind of touchstone in tracing that transformation.

The early Puritan communities were organic, tightly knit structures. The inhabitants were convinced that all men need direction in life. No single institution on earth was seen as possessing absolute sovereignty, of course; their intensely Protestant outlook forbade placing total trust in any human organization. Nevertheless, they believed that the various levels of the civil government did have basic responsibilities in regulating prices, the purchase of land, public utilities, and personal fashion. The minister might advise the public officials on such matters, but it was the political authorities who were seen as being ultimately responsible for their enforcement.

The Question of Status

In the mid-nineteenth century, the British scholar Sir Henry Maine characterized the coming of the modern world in terms of the concept, "from status to contract." Seventeenth-century New England fits this outline beautifully. Members of the first generation of Puritans (1630-60), as well as the second generation (1660-90), were deeply concerned about the threat posed by open, voluntary contracts to the received medieval world view. Considerations of status were paramount in their minds, and it became increasingly obvious to everyone concerned that the New World was not going to be a place in which inherited concepts of personal status were going to flourish. There was too much cheap land, too many economic alternatives, too many "callings" — occupations — for the survival of traditional status concepts.

The essence of the Puritan idea of status is found in the Larger Catechism of the Westminster Confession of Faith, that comprehensive body of theology hammered out by the Puritan scholars of Cromwell's England in the mid-1640's. The question of status was basic to the Puritans' interpretation of the Fifth

Commandment, "honor thy father and thy mother." The catechism reads: "By *father* and *mother*, in the fifth commandment, are meant not only natural parents, but all superiors in age and gifts; and especially such as, by God's ordinance, are over us in place of authority, whether in family, church, or commonwealth. . . . The general scope of the fifth commandment is the performance of those duties which we mutually owe in our several relations, as inferiors, superiors, or equals."[2]

There is nothing innately reprehensible in the idea that men should observe distinctions among each other; "civility" and basic etiquette have always required as much. The idea that superiors ("parents") have duties to inferiors ("children"), and vice versa, is common enough. When the Soviet Union in the early years of its history attempted to tamper with this principle in family life and in military affairs, the whole fabric of Russian life was disrupted, and these short-lived experiments in supposedly non-status society were abandoned for the sake of survival. Society never really faces the question of "status or no status," but only questions of what kind of status and the locus of authority in the enforcement of status distinctions. It was here that Puritan New England encountered its difficulties.

The Larger Catechism summarized the accepted status ethic of Puritan culture. Both superiors and inferiors were given positive injunctions and negative warnings about respecting the duties and obligations of authority and submission. Leaders are to expect the following from inferiors: reverence, respect, prayer, obedience, love, and honor. Inferiors are not to neglect their duties, rebel, curse, or mock their superiors. Superiors, on the other hand, owe their inferiors the following: love, prayer, counsel, rewards, chastening, protection. The sins of superiors are also listed: "an inordinate seeking of themselves, their own glory, ease, profit, or pleasure," and "inordinate" is understandably but unfortunately left undefined. Superiors are not to command

---

2. *Larger Catechism* (1647), answers 124, 126. I am using the standard edition published by the Free Presbyterian Church of Scotland (1970).

anything unlawful from their inferiors, or correct them unduly, or to lead them into temptation, "or any way dishonouring themselves, or lessening their authority, by an unjust, indiscreet, rigorous, or remiss behaviour."[3]

In a family, church, or voluntary society, these injunctions can be more easily applied. But the medieval perspective of the Puritans can be seen in their unwillingness to limit the locus of the term "family." They were intent upon transferring the status requirements of the family to the civil government.

The Familistic State

A family is a limited entity. Members are born into it and grow to maturity; eventually they die. Sons and daughters leave to form new families, and this alters the relationship between parents and children. Parents grow old and sometimes feeble, so they have an incentive to rear children competently; their own future survival may depend upon the maturity and faithfulness of the children. The parents therefore have an incentive to avoid keeping offspring in perpetual childhood. The relationships are intensely *personal*, and therefore bounded by feelings of love, honor, loyalty, and directly threatened by feelings of jealousy, disrespect, or hatred.

The civil government, however, is a completely different institution, established for different ends, and governed by different rules. Its function is not to father children, rear them, promote their maturity, or care for them. The state's function is to protect men against violence, both domestic and foreign. Invasions are to be repelled; thieves and bullies are to be restrained. The state is to be ruled by formal laws that are predictable, applying to all members of society.[4] By its very nature, it is an *impersonal* structure; it is not to respect persons in the administration of justice. Ideally, men are to be ruled by formal civil law,

---

3. *Ibid.*, ans. 127-130. Direct quote from #130.

4. F. A. Hayek, *The Constitution of Liberty* (Chicago: University of Chicago Press, 1960).

not by capricious men. Formal law is to restrain the activities of the state itself, limiting its arbitrariness.

A Hopeless Conflict of Interests and Lack of Harmony

In retrospect, it is not difficult for us to understand why the New England Puritans, no less than their English cousins, would find it difficult to assign limits to a familistic state. It is rather like children setting limits on fathers, especially when fathers confront their children not merely with the threat of violence, but also with the moral obligation of submission. Yet from the 1630's through the 1670's, this is precisely what Puritan leaders attempted to do. They wanted to permit godly men sufficient freedom to exercise their personal callings, for they well understood that if a man is personally responsible before God for his acts, he must be given wide latitude in exercising his personal talents without interference from other men, including leaders. Nevertheless, they also wanted to insure that the "family of God's people" would preserve its inherited status distinctions and also insure that peace and harmony would prevail as a testimony to the whole world. As the seventeenth century progressed, they were to find that the two goals were very frequently in opposition, and harmony was not maintained.

Modern commentators must be extremely careful not to read our contemporary views about status back into the seventeenth century – or at least not back into the first three quarters. There was no public outcry from "oppressed" inferiors, no colony-wide movement to redress grievances. There is little, if any, evidence that the "inferior sort" and their elected representatives, the deputies, were in fundamental opposition to the medieval view of status obligations. Puritan society was in reality a society made up of people who in England would have been regarded as the "middling sort" – sons of the lesser gentry, yeoman farmers, craftsmen, and others who had sufficient capital to make the journey. There were servants, however, and these could wind up as members of a truly lower class, but masters were expected (and even compelled legally) to provide some capital, usually in the form of tools and training, to departing indentured servants (who could be kept in service no more than seven years). Still, in every society there are higher and lower, richer and poorer, and the sumptuary legislation codified these distinctions. For many years, the subordinate population was willing to acquiesce in what the Larger Catechism required, an acknowledgement of their superiors "according to their several ranks, and the nature of their places."

The Sumptuary Codes

The Puritan magistrates concluded, as had leaders in European society for centuries, that it is not always easy to identify members of various classes. In New England, for all intents and purposes, there were three levels — higher, middle, lower — but the law codes only recognized two. Puritan legislation borrowed a practice of the most familistic of all state structures, the military: uniforms. The Larger Catechism listed as one of the duties of inferiors the "imitation of their [superiors'] virtues and graces," but no Puritan leader was so naive as to believe that such a requirement allowed the "inferior sort" to imitate their superiors' tastes in fashion. Thus, in 1651, both the magistrates and deputies of Massachusetts agreed on the following piece of legislation, one that is unrivaled in American history for its sheer medievalism — comprehensive, authoritarian, and thoroughly hierarchical.

Although several declarations and orders have been made by this Court against excess in apparel, both of men and of women, which have not yet taken that effect which were to be desired, but on the contrary we cannot but to our grief take notice that intolerable excesses and bravery have crept in upon us, and especially amongst the people of mean condition, to the dishonor of God, the scandal of our profession [i.e., profession of faith], the consumption of estates, and altogether we acknowledge it to be a matter of great difficulty, in regard to the blindness of men's minds and the stubbornness of their wills, to set down exact rules to confine all sorts of persons, yet we cannot but account it our duty to commend unto all sorts of persons a sober and moderate use of those blessings which, beyond our expectation, the LORD has been pleased to afford unto us in this wilderness, and also declare our utter detestation and dislike that men or women of mean condition, educations, and callings should take upon them the garb of gentlemen, by the wearing of gold or silver lace, or buttons, or points at their knees, to walk in great boots; or women of the same rank to wear tiffany hoods or scarves, which though allowable to persons of greater estates, or more liberal education, yet we cannot but judge it intolerable in persons of such like condition. . . .[5]

Unless a citizen was of a good education, or a military officer, or a civil officer, he could not wear such clothing unless his estate could be valued at 200 pounds or more, according to a "true and indifferent value." For a violation of this statute, a ten shilling fine was imposed.

A similar, though shorter, statute had been passed by the Connecticut authorities a decade earlier.[6] This should not be understood as an indication of Massachusetts' late arrival in the area of sumptuary legislation. The wearing of lace by social inferiors had been the subject of at least two pieces of Massachusetts legislation in the 1630's. It was only to be used as a small edging (presumably only by the upper classes), and lace in general was prohibited from being worn extensively on any garment.[7] Special import taxes were placed on luxury items, "for preventing the immoderate expense of provisions brought from beyond the seas." Such goods as sugar, spice, wine, and tobacco were included. The tariff was 16 percent for direct purchasers and 33 percent of the import price for retailers (thus making it more difficult for local retailers to compete in sales with the more distant, and presumably less compelling, London merchants).[8]

---

5. *Mass. Col. Recs.*, III, p. 243.

6. J. Hammond Trumball and Charles Hoadly (eds.), *The Public Records of the Colony of Connecticut* (New York: AMS Press, [1850-90] 1968), I (1641), p. 64. [Cited hereafter as *Conn. Col. Recs.*]

7. *Mass. Col. Recs.*, I (1635), p. 183; (1639), pp. 274-75.

8. *Ibid.*, I (1636), p. 186.

Tobacco consumption, which was regarded by Puritan leaders as another unnecessary excess, had been under fire [sorry, I couldn't resist] from some of the directors of the Massachusetts Bay Company right from its inception.[9] All four of the Puritan commonwealths – Massachusetts, New Haven, Connecticut, and Plymouth – passed numerous provisions placing restrictions on the sale and consumption of the "noxious weed." These prohibitions were not really status oriented; they were motivated by a number of fears. One, understandably, was fire. Boston was forever burning down in the seventeenth century, as Carl Bridenbaugh's *Cities in the Wilderness* reports in some detail. At one stage, Massachusetts prohibited the buying and selling of tobacco entirely, although it was legal to import it for re-export later.[10] They apparently thought it was all right to burn down other cities, if local merchants were to gain some profit in the transaction. Plymouth tried to ban its importation in 1641, but repealed the law six months later.[11] Connecticut's ban is the most amusing in retrospect. It was directly tied to the issue of personal health, but in the exact opposite of today's concern: no one under the age of twenty who had not already addicted himself to tobacco was allowed to buy it, unless he had a physician's certificate "that it is useful to him," and he had to present the certificate to the Court in order to obtain a license to purchase the weed.[12]

Time-Wasting

Taverns, brewers, and liquor retailers were under restrictions throughout the century. Indeed, some of these controls are as common today as they were in the New England colonies. Men were not to waste precious time in taverns, the magistrates

----

9. *Ibid.*, I, pp. 387-89, 403.

10. *Ibid.*, I (1635), p. 136; (1635), p. 180.

11. Nathaniel B. Shurtleff (ed.), *Records of the Colony of New Plymouth* (New York: AMS Press, [1855] 1968), XI, p. 38. [Cited hereafter as *Plym. Col. Recs.*]

12. *Conn. Col. Recs.*, I (1647), p. 153.

believed, so they went to considerable lengths to protect men from their own weaknesses. Then, as now, *licensing* was the primary means of control, and it was equally a source of public revenue. The annual licensing of taverns, said the Massachusetts magistrates, is inescapable, "Seeing it is difficult to order and keep the houses of public entertainment in such conformity to the wholesome laws established by this Court as is necessary for the prevention of drunkenness, excessive drinking, vain expense of money, time, and the abuse of the creatures of God. . . ."[13]

Although it seems incredible today, shuffleboard was regarded as a prime danger. There were not to be scenes of elderly men spending a leisurely afternoon in the park playing this devil's game. Such games were a sign of idling — a waste of God's most precious resource, time — and they were especially prohibited in taverns and when practiced by servants and youths. The magistrates were willing to go to real extremes to stamp out games of chance and shuffleboard.[14] These regulations extended throughout the century, unlike virtually all other sumptuary laws, indicating a continuity of opinion against "vain pursuits." (It might be said that at least in New England, shuffleboard was not to be an old man's pastime because old men were always regarded as fully productive until they grew feeble; if a man could work, he was expected to. If shuffleboard drew the wrath of Puritan magistrates, Leisure World or Sun City or retirement centers in Florida would have been regarded by them as nothing short of satanic — the worst sort of wastefulness of men's productive capacities.)

As in so many other cases, one colony did not participate in the sumptuary mania: Rhode Island.[15] But Rhode Island was

---

13. *Mass. Col. Recs.*, IV, pt. I (1654), p. 287.

14. *Mass. Col. Recs.*, II, pp. 180, 195; III, p. 102; IV, pt. I, p. 20; *Con. Col. Recs.*, I, p. 289; *Plym. Col. Recs.*, XI, p. 66.

15. On Rhode Island's absence of sumptuary legislation, see William B. Weeden, *Economic and Social History of New England, 1620-1789*, 2 vols. (New York: Hillary House, [1890] 1963), I, p. 290. Weeden provides a summary of the various sumptuary statutes: pp. 226ff.

not a Puritan commonwealth. Its founder, Roger Williams, had argued for the separation of church and state — not primarily to protect the state, but to protect the church!

The Problem of Social Mobility

The Puritans' emphasis on personal responsibility, thrift, hard work, the moral righteousness of all lawful occupations, careful accounting (moral and financial), honest dealing, the fulfillment of contracts, and their concern with the future, both heavenly and (especially from 1630-60) earthly, all combined to provide an atmosphere conducive to economic growth and personal wealth. Another important feature of Puritan thought that has seldom been recognized is the antipathy of Puritan preachers to the sin of envy. Samuel Willard, whose two decades of Sunday evening sermons on the Larger Catechism, *A Compleat Body of Divinity* (1726), stands as the *Summa* of Puritan theology, saw envy as a direct violation of the law of God. He set forth this standard to his congregation: they "ought not to envy, but to rejoice in the prosperity of their neighbors."[16] Willard's lengthy attack on the sin of envy stood as one of the longest expositions on the subject in English until the publication in 1966 of Prof. Helmut Schoeck's crucial study, *Envy: A Theory of Social Behavior*.[17] Cotton Mather agreed entirely with Willard's analysis: "It will have no good aspect upon us, if it should be so, that a leveling spirit gets so much head among us, that no man shall be in anything superior to his neighbors, but his very superiority shall make him obnoxious to envious indignities. . . ."[18]

Envy, as Schoeck has argued so incisively, restricts the incentives for and impetus to economic development. First, it discourages the free discussion among members of a society of a basic

---

16. Samuel Willard, *A Compleat Body of Divinity* (New York: Johnson Reprints, [1726] 1969), p. 644. This was the largest book ever published in the colonies in its day — close to one million words.

17. Helmut Schoeck, *Envy: A Theory of Social Behavior* (New York: Harcourt, Brace, [1966] 1970).

18. Cotton Mather, *Concio ad Populum* (1719), p. 18.

fact of life: *time*. Men do not discuss their personal futures if their goal is to *conceal* their aspirations, fortunes, and plans. Yet they must conceal such matters in a society motivated by feelings of envy. Second, under such restraints, innovations are unlikely, since no one wants to let his neighbors see how much better off a person is as a result of some advance.[19] Cut off discussion of the future, compromise men's orientation toward the future, penalize advancement technologically and personally, and the society in question will show few signs of economic growth.[20]

Personal and Social Growth

Puritan preaching, therefore, served as a stimulus to both personal wealth in one's calling and economic development for the community. Men were to be moderate in all things, and they were not to pursue wealth for its own sake. This was made clear by a century of preaching, from John Cotton to Cotton Mather to Benjamin Franklin. Nevertheless, there is nothing innately wrong with wealth in the Puritan view, however much a spiritual snare and delusion great wealth might become. So when men began to follow the tenets of the Puritan faith, they found themselves steadily increasing in wealth, both personally and culturally. This was to raise an absolutely baffling dilemma: how was the fact of social mobility to be reconciled with medieval categories of fixed status, implying defined place and function?

The Puritans were hardly the first people to face this dilemma. The millennium of institutional struggles over monastic reform in the Roman Catholic Church testifies to the traditional nature of the problem. From the day that St. Benedict set forth his eminently practical monastic rules — humility, hard work, thrift, patience, self-help, discipline — the monasteries that followed his guide faced the problem of economic growth. The monasteries had a tendency to get richer and richer. Then the

---

19. Schoeck, *Envy*, pp. 46-50.

20. On the importance of future-orientation to economic and cultural life, see Edward C. Banfield, *The Unheavenly City: The Nature and Future of Our Urban Crisis* (Boston: Little, Brown & Co., 1969).

original ideal of personal poverty was abandoned by certain abbots and monks, and pressures for reform came from the outside.[21] This pattern prevailed right down into the sixteenth century, when Henry VIII confiscated monastic property in the name of a higher morality.

In 1632, it was one thing for Gov. John Winthrop to challenge Thomas Dudley with respect to the latter's ostentation in adorning his home with wainscoting (a wooden paneling on the walls of a house). He had more justification, given Puritan standards, for such an act, for it was, in his words, "the beginning of a plantation."[22] Even so, it is not hard to understand Dudley's anger when Winthrop had the frame of his house removed. Dudley — who was to alternate with Winthrop as the Governor of Massachusetts Bay in the early years, and who regarded himself as the stricter Puritan of the two — objected, and Winthrop, in his own words, "acknowledged himself faulty" in taking this responsibility on himself without having consulted with other magistrates.[23] But after half a century had elapsed, we find ministers using the same old "wilderness condition"[24] argument — the spiritual wilderness analogous to the Israelites' wanderings — in order to justify the intervention of the civil government in community fashions. Sermons delivered in the second generation of New England (1660-90) would dwell on the graciousness of God in making New England into a fruitful land, and a little later would revert to the older "wilderness" theme. It is unlikely that any newly rich citizen of Boston or some

21. Cf. Dom Cuthbert Butler, *Benedictine Monachism* (2nd ed.; London: Longmans, Green & Co., 1924), pp. 150-55. St. Benedict was totally opposed to private ownership among the monks: *The Rule of St. Benedict* (Westminster, Maryland: Newman Press, 1952), pp. 85, 87, 127.

22. James K. Hosmer (ed.), *Winthrop's Journal: "History of New England,"* 1630-1649 (New York: Barnes & Noble, [1908] 1966), I, p. 77.

23. *Ibid.*, I, pp. 84-85.

24. Perry Miller, *Errand Into the Wilderness* (New York: Harper Torchbooks, [1956] 1964), ch. 1; Peter N. Carroll, *Puritanism and the Wilderness: The Intellectual Significance of the New England Frontier, 1629-1700* (New York: Columbia University Press, 1969).

optimistic social climber would conclude that his, or his wife's, style of dress in some mysterious way constituted a grave deviation from a hypothetical "wilderness standard" of clothing — not in 1680, at least.

Unprecedented Mobility

The very success of the Puritans in overcoming the limitations of a wilderness disrupted the accepted medieval tradition of fixed or semi-fixed status distinctions. The rapidity of social change and the fluidity of social mobility baffled Puritan ministers. By medieval standards, the social mobility was unprecedented and incomprehensible. This was especially true of Boston, which was becoming the major port in the colonies. It was a society in which a former indentured servant could become a ship owner or a wealthy skilled craftsman. John Hull, one of the most respected men in New England, and surely one of the richest, had raised himself from very modest circumstances.[25] How was a magistrate to determine someone's social status, except in cases of extreme poverty or wealth?

Social status became as much of a problem for the second generation as the administration of a "just price" had been for the first. It was an elusive quality, even as the just price had been an elusive quantity, which refused to be catalogued or defined in written legislation. Yet it seemed as though this very *elusiveness* hypnotized Puritan preachers. They were certain that a proper definition could be found, but the perverse changes going on in New England society kept it concealed. In their eyes, the evil lay with the overly fluid society and not with the lack of rigor in the definition of status. Changes in fashion, imitation by members of the lower classes of their social superiors, the increasing affluence of the lower class as a class, this seemingly perverse unwillingness of men to keep in their original stations into which they had been born: here were signs of despair.

---

25. Samuel Eliot Morison, *Builders of the Bay Company* (Boston: Houghton Mifflin, 1930), ch. 5.

Puritan commentators were convinced that New England society was in the process of dissolution; God was about to depart from the land.

Puritan Preaching Against Pride and Ambition

By 1674, Cotton Mather's father, Increase Mather, was convinced that the continual violation of the Fifth Commandment — the status commandment — was the chief sin of his generation. (That someone named Increase could take this position only serves to emphasize the irony.) Inferiors were rising up against superiors in the commonwealth — in families, schools, churches. It was not an uprising that he feared, but this incessant rising *up*. "If there be any prevailing iniquity in New England, this is it . . . And mark what I say, if ever New England be destroyed, this very sin of disobedience to the fifth commandment will be the ruin of the land."[26] Samuel Willard agreed with Mather.[27]

The problem, as the Puritan divines saw it, was that men were not satisfied with their lot in life. Daniel Denison's last sermon, appended by another famous preacher of his day, William Hubbard, to Hubbard's funeral sermon for Denison, cites ambition as the curse of the land, along with envy: ". . . Ambition is restless, must raise commotions, that thereby it might have an opportunity of advancement, and employ envy to depress others, that they fancy may stand in their way. . . ."[28] Such ambitious men are unwilling "to abide in the calling, wherein they are set; they cannot stay for the blessing, nor believe when God hath need of their service, he will find them an employment, whatever stands in the way of their design, must give place. . . ."[29]

---

26. Increase Mather, *The Wicked Man's Portion* (1675), p. 17. Preached in 1674.

27. Samuel Willard, *Useful Instructions for a Professing People in Times of Great Security and Degeneracy* (1673), p. 75.

28. Daniel Denison, *Irenicon*, attached to William Hubbard, *The Benefit of a Well-ordered Conversation* (1684), p. 195.

29. *Ibid.*, p. 196.

The clergy's practical problem was obvious: assigning explicit guidelines that would help the magistrate to decide in any given case whether a man's ambition was of the "restless" sort or whether the individual was simply exercising newly discovered personal talents in some new calling. To argue, as Denison did, that a fixed calling is basic to God's plan of salvation for each saint, involved him in a form of feudalism-manorialism that was unlikely to survive the acids of the competitive market mechanism, with its concept of voluntary free labor, the right of private contract, and profit in terms of an impersonal price mechanism.

The Boston Synod of 1679 listed pride in apparel and the unwarranted imitation by servants of the dress of their superiors as early entries in its catalogue of over a dozen social evils that had brought miseries to New England.[30] Five years earlier, Increase Mather himself had announced the difficulty of distinguishing the dress of the regenerate from that of the unregenerate. It is a dark day when "professors of religion fashion themselves according to the world."[31] But given the inescapable and undeniable existence of human sin, what could be done to correct this problem? What *are* the standards of legitimate fashion for a godly society? Are they subject to change? Like the standards of economic oppression, the just price, and usurious interest, the standards of godly fashion were elusive.

Strange Apparel

Rev. Urian Oakes struggled mightily with this difficulty. He was convinced that human pride expresses itself in outward garb, "in affected trimmings and adornings of the outward man, that body of clay that is going to the dust and worms." Strange apparel is going to be punished, he said, citing Zephaniah 1:8 as proof. Yet some rich and lovely garments are all right (II Samuel 1:24):

---

30. Boston Synod, *The Necessity of Reformation* (1679), pp. 2-3.
31. Increase Mather, *The Day of Trouble Is Near* (1674), p. 22.

Nor am I so severe, or morose, as to exclaim against this or that fashion, provided it carry nothing of immodesty in it, or contrarily to the rules of moral honesty. The civil custom of the place where we live is that which we must regulate in this case. But when persons spend more time in trimming their bodies than their souls. . . . When they go beyond what their state and condition will allow, that they are necessitated to run into debt, and neglect the works of mercy and charity, or exact upon others in their dealings, that they may maintain their port and garb; or when they exceed their rank and degree (whereas one end of apparel is to distinguish and put a difference between persons according to their places and conditions) and when the sons and daughters of Sion are proud and haughty in their carriage and attire in an humbling time, when the church is brought low, Jerusalem and Judah are in a ruinous condition, and the LORD calls to deep humiliation: This is very displeasing to God, and both Scripture and Reason condemn it.[32]

Oakes was preaching to the magistrates of the colony, in a 1673 election sermon, an annual ritual that helped to bridge the gap between church and state. But he did not go into specific details concerning the nature of the required legislation – election sermons almost never did – and so nothing was put into operation.

Oakes had put most of the Puritan theologians' opposition to the flux of modern life into one lengthy exposition. Excessive social change breaks down familiar communal standards, which in turn are supposed to help preserve members of differing classes in traditional occupations and in dress reflecting those occupations. The hierarchy of medieval life – a hierarchy reflecting a great chain of being from God to Satan – was being shattered by the winds of change. Men and women were increasingly unwilling in the late seventeenth century to accept the limitations of such arbitrary status concepts of the exercise of their property rights.

What was "civil custom"? In a society which had grown from

---

32. Urian Oakes, *New-England Pleaded With* (1673), p. 34. An election sermon delivered in Boston in May, 1673.

a tiny, rural colony in an uncharted wilderness to a thriving and productive component of a newly developed English trade system, civil custom was indeed the question. Customs were anything but fixed or universal. After 1680, clerical opinion no longer carried as much weight in establishing or maintaining older customs. The very fluidity of fashion, where new styles could sweep through the community, reflected the lack of fixed standards, and this fact dismayed the preachers.

Conclusion

Status distinctions were supposed to be respected by members of a Holy Commonwealth; this meant that each status required its appropriate fashions, manners, customs. The problem which the first generation had never been willing to consider was to make itself felt in the 1670's. In a society in which men are not only free to increase their estates, but in fact have a moral obligation to do so, should men not be allowed to improve their social statuses? If Puritan frugality, the rational use of time and resources, systematic accounting, personal responsibility, and a future-oriented view of the world are allowed to combine into an ethos favoring both individual and aggregate economic growth, then social mobility, upward or downward, should be characteristic of that society. Yet the Puritan theologians of the second generation did not reach such a conclusion. Therefore, given their unwillingness to accept the legitimacy of social mobility on such a scale, they had an obligation to spell out the nature of specific legislation, both ecclesiastical and civil, that would define the relationship between status and wealth, and between status and fashion. This was the great stumbling stone for the Puritan oligarchs. The ministers were never able to agree on such rules. The sumptuary laws went unenforced, relics of the first generation's confidence in status legislation. Fashions continued to degenerate, and finally, to the horror of many of the pastors, Puritan saints began wearing wigs! As far as the sermons of the 1670's are concerned, Worthington C. Ford's description holds good: "Massachusetts Bay was becoming degenerate, the older generation said. It is always becoming degenerate."[33] By the 1680's, the civil magistrates had abandoned the attempt to maintain medieval concepts of social status in an increasingly modern culture.

The older Puritan standards of social propriety had become the victims, not of Enlightenment rationalism or philosophical skepticism, but of operational Puritanism. Like the medieval monasteries, the Puritan commonwealth had prospered as a direct result of Puritan teachings. But unlike the monasteries, the society of late-seventeenth-century New England did not heed the call to reform itself. Indeed, the cries for reform were so vague, especially after the defeat of the Indians in King Philip's War (1675-76), that had any magistrate wanted to listen, he would have had nothing to hear in the way of specific reforms. The saints in the churches were as unwilling to abide by the older standards of dress and social status as those outside the churches who had neglected to "own the covenant" of church membership. Puritan sermons had warned of God's wrath in the face of hardheartedness, but when judgment came—in the shape of an Indian uprising—the Puritan military forces were victorious. Success was the one thing that the pessimistic jeremiad sermons of the second generation simply could not deal with successfully.

33. Worthington C. Ford, "Sewall and Noyes on Wigs," *Publications of the Colonial Society of Massachusetts*, XX (1917-19), p. 112.

Conclusion

When the Puritans arrived in New England, they possessed a vision of the biblical city on a hill that would serve as a beacon to Europe in all its degradation. They would conquer the wilderness[1] and establish a Holy Commonwealth for all to see and imitate. Only if they broke their covenant with God — which was always possible and a great temptation[2] — would their experiment fail. This optimism concerning their potential future, if they remained faithful to God, was part of their covenantal view of society. Godly men would learn to govern themselves in terms of God's law. They would be aided in this task by the hierarchical covenantal institutions of society — family, church, and civil government — which would also rule in terms of God's revealed law, executing God's judgments faithfully. Each resident of the commonwealth would be offered the blessings of righteousness under God. The Puritans expected to see God's blessings among them in response to their covenantal faithfulness.

But they had a major problem. They had to decide just what it was that God required of them in every area of life, including economics. What is God's law? How can it be applied in historic circumstances? How could they operate in this world while remaining faithful to the perfect law of a heavenly God? This is

---

1. Peter N. Carroll, *Puritanism and the Wilderness: The Intellectual Significance of the New England Frontier, 1629-1700* (New York: Columbia University Press, 1969).

2. Sacvan Bercovich, *The American Jeremiad* (Madison: University of Wisconsin Press, 1978), ch. 1.

what Edmund S. Morgan has called the Puritan dilemma: ". . . to found a society where the perfection of God would find proper recognition among imperfect men."[3] They carried with them the intellectual baggage of the early scholastic traditions. Had they adopted instead the free market views of the later Spanish scholastics, the history of the first fifty years of New England would have been very different. They would have avoided the endless economic disruptions caused by the government's attempt to impose medieval economic controls on a Puritan commonwealth.

The second generation did reject the bulk of their fathers' scholastic economic views after 1676, but this was not the result of their having rethought the principles of economics from a biblical point of view. It was the result of a new pietism, the steady abandoning of the original covenantal idea. They no longer understood how Old Testament laws could be successfully applied in New England in order to build a Holy Commonwealth. They abandoned the task of constructing the city on a hill by means of biblical law. This marked the beginning of the end of the Puritan experiment in New England, including the economic experiments.

In this loss of faith they were not alone.[4] Religious pietism was sweeping the Western world after 1660, in England, the Continent, and the Puritan colonies. The former confidence in the future about the possibilities for the expansion of God's external kingdom — cultural, social, and political — had faded. Louis XIV, Charles II, and other secular monarchs were no longer interested in the expansion of the kingdom of God, but rather with their own political kingdoms. A religious pessimism concerning the external affairs of the world set in for the next eight decades in New England, from 1660 until the Great Awakening of the 1740's, and in this later incarnation, postmillennial

---

3. Edmund S. Morgan, *The Puritan Dilemma: The Story of John Winthrop* (Boston: Little, Brown, 1958), p. 155.

4. William M. Lamont, *Godly Rule: Politics and Religion, 1603-60* (London: Macmillan, 1969).

optimism was self-consciously separated from biblical law. The explicit antinomianism of the Great Awakening destroyed the last traces of the Holy Commonwealth ideal.[5] But that tombstone was built over a vision that was long-since moribund. By 1680, Puritan theologians and preachers knew that in all likelihood, their hopes concerning the Holy Commonwealth were not going to be realized.

Cultural and economic Puritanism, however, still operated, but on a private level. Individual saints saved, planned, and built for the future. The Holy Commonwealth, while not so holy as it had been in 1630, was more mature. It had freed men from many of the shackles that had bound them for a thousand years. A new land was ready for the application of Puritan hard work and thrift. Political institutions, built as they were on the doctrine of the priesthood of all believers and the validity of covenants, provided the democratic mechanism for orderly transfers of political power. Economic institutions, built in terms of individual responsibility before God, now helped to release the energies of a diligent community of citizens. The old Puritan mistrust of concentrated political power, when coupled with the old medieval tradition of localism, created a hitherto unheard of economic freedom. What was socially inoperative in Puritanism had been largely scrapped by a later generation of Puritans. What remained was to stand as part of the foundation of the American republic.

---

5. Richard L. Bushman, *From Puritan to Yankee: Character and the Social Order in Connecticut, 1690-1765* (New York: Norton, [1967] 1970).

SUBJECT INDEX

63